Eco Love

Earth Day, Environment Awareness Coloring Book

Mother Earth Patterns, Save The Planet Designs & Slogans For Kids & Adults

Rachel Mintz

D1613683

Copyright © 2020 Palm Tree Publishing - All rights reserved. No part of this publication may be reproduced, distributed, or transmitted in any form or by any means, including photocopying, recording, or other electronic or mechanical methods, without the prior written permission of the publisher, except in the case of brief quotations embodied in critical reviews and certain other noncommercial uses permitted by copyright law. Images used under license from Shutterstock.com

Colors Testing Page

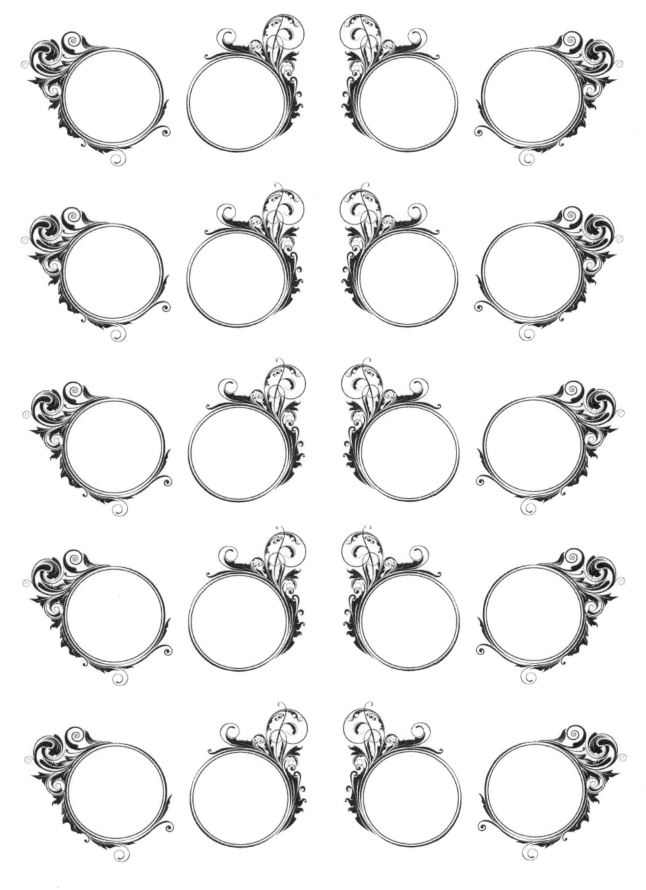

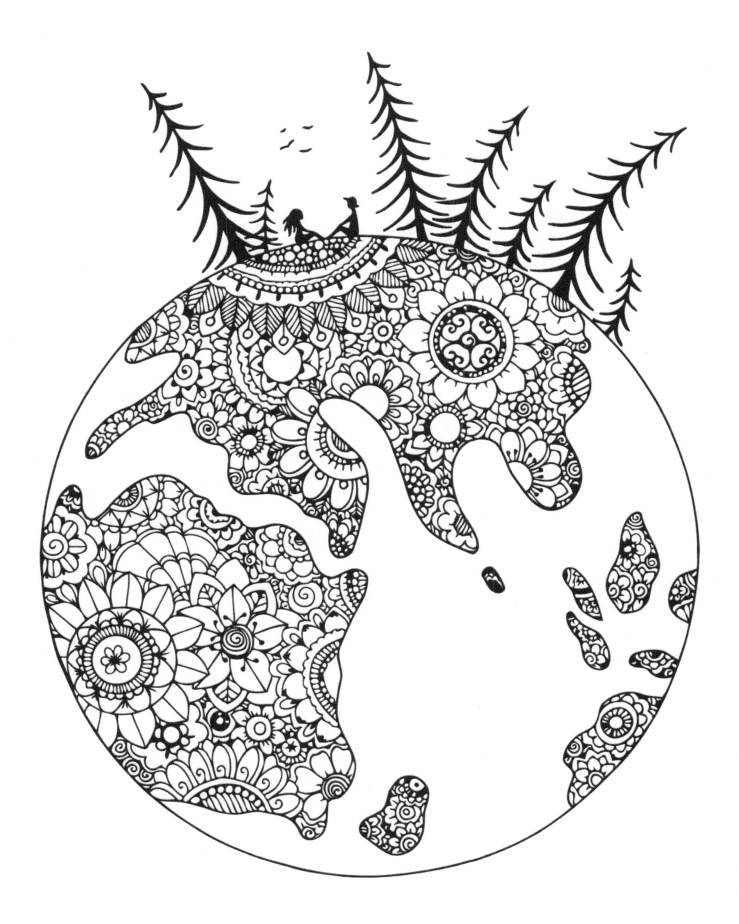

Think Blue and Go Green

Save the Sea to See the Future

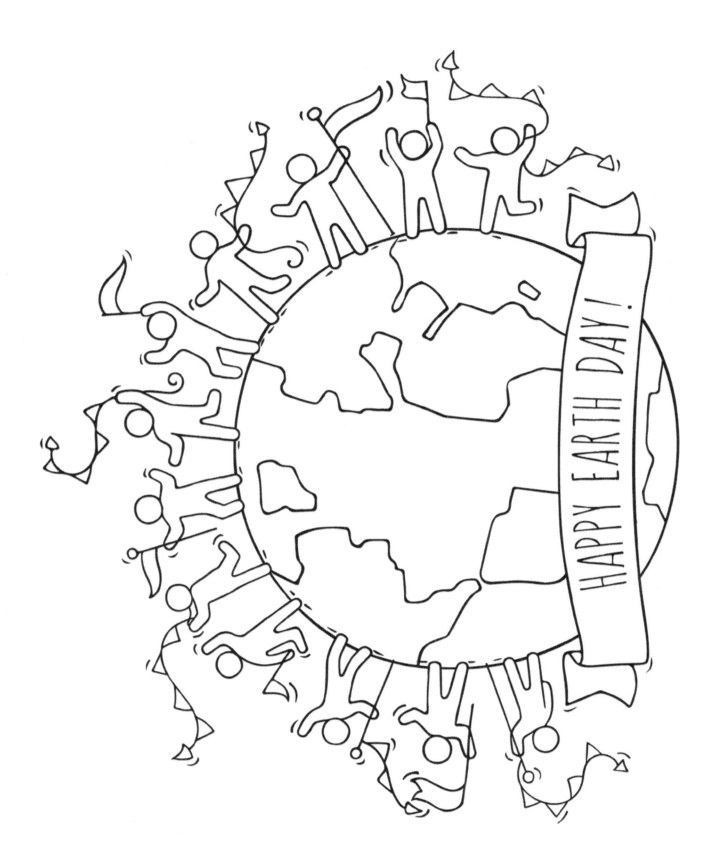

Save The Ocean

No water, no life.
No blue, no green

Save The Ocean

My Memories

Thank you for coloring with us

Please review THIS book

More RACHEL MINTZ Coloring Books For You at Amazon:

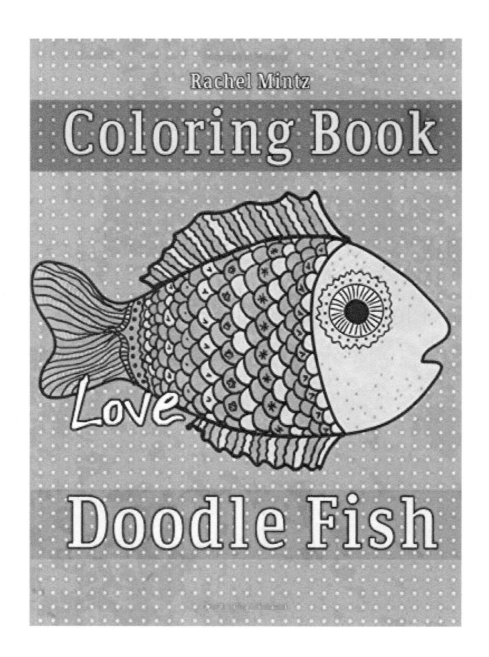

Scan below to order from Amazon

RACHEL MINTZ Coloring Books

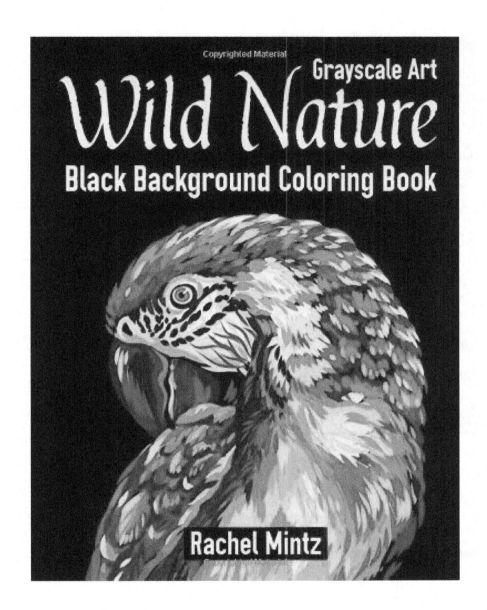

Scan below to order from Amazon

RACHEL MINTZ Coloring Books

Scan below to order from Amazon

RACHEL MINTZ Coloring Books

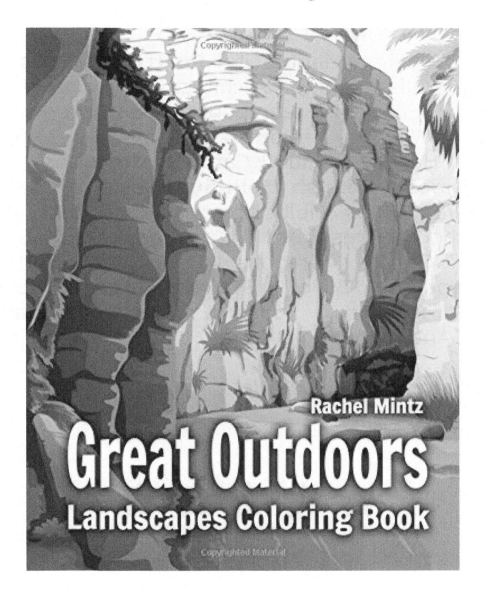

Scan below to order from Amazon

Look for more RACHEL MINTZ coloring books at Amazon.

Mandalas | Wildlife | Marine Life| **Portraits** | Dogs | Cats | **Flowers** | Skulls | Gothic | Architecture | Romantic | Texts & Sayings | Ethnic | Steampunk | **Fashion** | Horses | Unicorns | Witches | Horror | Grayscale | Sports | Christmas | Holidays | Kids | Cars | **Motorbikes** | Trucks | Urban | Fairies | **Jewish Holidays**: Passover, Hanukkah, Purim | Safari | Pets |Multicultural | Educational for Kids | Back to School | **Preschool & Toddlers** | Army & Military | Knights & Castles | Dragons | Princesses | Butterflies | Birds | Reptiles | Bible | **Stained Glass** | Abstract | Machines | **Robots** | Space & Science | **Zombies** | Monsters | And many more topics..

Search Amazon for 'Rachel Mintz

Thank you for coloring with us

We will be very thankful if you could take a minute to review THIS book

Made in the USA
Middletown, DE
22 April 2023

29306508R00044